INDESTRUCTIBLE

CRISTY C. ROAD

D1377113

INDESTRUCTIBLE

Written and Illustrated by Cristy C. Road
Edited by Chris Terry

Inspired by teenage rabble rousers, charming sluts, daunting bastards, high school, Miami, Cuba, and early nineties punk rock.

All the stories in this book have happened before, although they arent documented in chronological order. If they were, different points that are trying to get conveyed might not make sense- So deal with it. Also, the names have been changed to protect the identities of the guilty, innocent, dirty, and prude.

You can find Cristy C. Road and all her other projects at

CROADCORE
c/o Cristy C. Road
PO Box 60169
Brooklyn, NY 11206
www.croadcore.org
croadcore@yahoo.com

First Edition - April 2006 - 3,000 copies
Second Edition - April 2008 - 3,000 copies

ISBN # 0-9770557-7-9
This is Microcosm Publishing # 76036

Microcosm Publishing
www.microcosmpublishing.com

INDESTRUCTIBLE

CRISTY C. ROAD

To me, adolescence was the time when we all knew
who we were. We knew enough to accomplish self-
righteousness. We knew we talked the wrong way, had
unkempt style, and smelled janky as hell. However.
in the eyes of our math teachers, our best friend's
parents, and sometimes our own parents; we were
hinging on self-destruction, no matter who we
were. And while they would push the envelope on
criticism and demonize our culture;
we were still something.

We were everything everyone didnt want us to be.

Because side-stepping the status-quo wouldnt
get us anywhere, right?
Yeah. Right.

Yami
Del Pino

Selene
Diaz

Eddy Edge
Echeverria

Marietta
Gomez

Julian M.
Gonzalez

Tess N.
Juan

1K Jones
Lombardi

Desiree C.
Marquez

Gustavo
Mendez

Eugene Skuz
Ramirez

Cristy C.
Road

Angelina L.
Ventura

ONE

It was my birthday and a six-foot long table stretched across the grass. It covered half the backyard, and while some of us could hardly navigate our bodies through the foliage, it was the only kind of table that could hold three styrofoam trays of maduros, morros, and paella. Everyone was wearing gold jewelry and either spandex biker shorts or acid wash denim pants. My body was sprouting terrestrial bumps and hairs that year- I was turning eleven that day. I remember being asked to tuck in my t-shirt and wipe the dog shit off my knees- it's what any self-respecting pubescent Cuban girl should do. Especially when around members of the opposite sex who are a few months shy of adolescence. However, I chose to perpetuate unruliness. I played soccer, ate my mother's friend's leftovers out of the trash, and hung live reptiles from my earlobes. That day I fell on the ground, and upon looking up, a seven year old boy perched himself beside me, and tilted his head in curiosity.

"Are you a boy or a girl?" he asked.

"I'm a girl." I responded. "Why do you care?"

"Oh, cause you look like a boy."

I wasn't sure if I was stoked about my androgyny. Two years back, lacking femininity gave me a positive spirit. Nevertheless, I would often ask myself if the forms my body was naturally shaping itself into was a slight message saying I should want to be a girl. I asked a friend of my mother's about this and she romanticized ovulating, pubic hair, and smells that encircled pussy, more so than dirt.

"Girl, you'll be a woman soon." She slouched towards me.

"But I don't want to be a woman."

"Oh come on, you know you can't wait to get your nails all done, get your hair done all nice, get yourself a boyfriend."

"That totally sounds like hell."

"That's only what you say now, I promise."

At times I wondered if I had to be a woman. Something in me anticipated growing up without submitting to what most people expected from me. Still, I sometimes entertained notions of the varied routes a growing teenager could choose. I flirted with the notion of having a best friend who felt like as much of a misfit as me. I flirted with thoughts of being tall and curvaceous, and trading in my Aerosmith cassette tapes for salsa music. I would be sexy. But at that moment, I wanted to grow with the facets I already knew, more so than grow by way of the rules pressed upon my gender. I wanted to go out late at night and drink beer. I wanted to wear overalls and dye my hair green. I wanted to talk about sex and stop pretending that I didn't know what an orgasm was. I wanted to be who I was in my pre-pubescent fantasies. I wanted to be a teenage boy.

I had one eyebrow stretched across my forehead . I only wore frayed denim and flannel, and I felt fine. Not because it was appropriate clothing for Miami's pit-stain climate - but because that year I developed interests, tastes, and an identity. To many, we were fools and eccentrics. To my heroes and likeminded individuals, we were artists and dreamers. Weathered fabrics and torn seams were a badge of honor. At twelve years old, I knew the words to almost every song on Metallica's **Master of Puppets** and that was totally empowering. How valuable was it memorize your favorite songs instead of the information you had to learn for Friday's math test? Very valuable.

Part of me knew I would be okay, even if I didn't have best friends and I was mostly uncomfortable in my own skin. I was excited about things like school. Not because I enjoyed the work- but because of the potential for interactions outside of the neighborhood that sheltered my family.

My family was made up of three women, a stanch work ethic, and a love for gardening and Spanish TV. We lived in a Latino community in Miami where every surrounding element stressed Cuban values, from meals to language. Lefty white ideas hinged on my taste, but were unheard of in my home. Ideas like vegetarianism and resisting beauty standards only existed in white America. My family anticipated growing curvaceous, because our beauty standard didn't comply with thinness. We anticipated mimicing the cultural doctrine of Cuba, rather than America. We sautéed everything in pork. But at the same time, it was safe to admit that white american culture tampers with every boundary in United States cities. While cultural preservation fortified us, popular culture tortured us. I respected the need my family felt to surround me with this Latina identity, and with that self-determination, I knew where I came from. But I was unsure as to what would define my appearance, my questionable optimism, and my uneasy method of growing up. I was unsure at what part white culture would torture me, and what ideals, unheard of to the Cuban family, would embrace me. And the enticement of adolescence went beyond any new pubes and first kisses.

On my first year of junior high, I grew tits. I would smile at the prospect of what they could do for me in the future, but right then, I just wanted to get high and cut them off. I didn't wanna submit to the changes that a girl is often taught to experience. Albeit, chances of single-handedly altering socialization are often bleak. While I didn't know how to shave and had crusty knots falling beside my shoulders- the questioning and self-doubt was unwavering. I had begun looking like a girl, but I developed a means to fight it. To fight an interest in walking upright and wearing short skirts. To fight against feeling like I should bare an interest in cosmetics and the boys everyone wanted to fuck. To fight the need of deodorizing my pussy and my human stench. But to a coming of age girl, was this okay? My mother thought it was- she thought the mainstream made girls submissive in nature and catty in persona. Either way, I experimented for a week or two. I masturbated to a Bobby Brown music video and threw myself a birthday party.

It was the kind that girls would wanna shave their thighs for behind their mothers' backs. In my culture, shaved thighs were for sluts. Although, In adolescent culture- who doesn't want to be a slut? My party would attract the kids everyone at school wanted to tongue or look like. I bought a Bobby Brown CD to play as dance music, and invited the girls at school who already looked like women and often felt sorry for me.

"What kinds of things are you going to have at your party?" One girl asked.

"I bought TLC and Bobby Brown CDs and a cake. My sister recorded a C+C Music Factory music video. I heard it's fucking dope."

"Why do you always have to say fuck?" One girl said.
"Are there gonna be guys there?" Another girl said.
"I guess." Inside, I wasn't into it.

On the eve of my party, I was hardly enthused, but convinced I was finally doing the right thing. That afternoon, I wasn't surprised to see that the only guests at my party were family members, some neighbor kid, and my fucking cake. I locked myself in my room, masturbated for the sixteenth time that day, and thought about how Aerosmith would have dealt with their adolescence. I stared at the wall and thought out loud.
"No one came to my party, my family's broke, I don't have a dad to be masculine with, but I have a sweet dog. I guess I'm not them." I thought "But us."

For a minute, I thought about dying. "Isn't it easier to just die sometimes?" I thought loudly, to the dismay of my dog. I crawled into the formica cabinet and swiped my index finger along the rim of a bottle of amonia. "Adulthood" I thought to myself. "I'll try to make it there, I guess. It seems to be a relatively interesting place." My thoughts on death, for once, digressed. "I'll be a luminary." I closed the bottle of amonia. "Like Steven Tyler from Aerosmith."

For once, I replaced the common self-pity with brilliance and determination to show a slew of popular teenagers that they can never match up to a strung-out, angst-ridden daughter of a Cuban feminist. This was junior high.
The following day I heard rumors that I had invited those girls because I was a dyke. According to other students, I clearly just wanted to fuck them. Albeit, I didn't think about queerness then, besides the times I rubbed one out in the shower thinking about girls in slips and combat boots.

That afternoon I sat by Eugene. Eugene was Colombian, tall and unearthly. He sat in the back of the room and played the noble part of class clown. His name was a staple in the school's drug culture because he dealt incredibly cheap weed. He was the oldest student in the eighth grade. Despite the stigma that existed on dealers and clowns, Eugene was soft spoken and intelligent. He was the first teenager I had ever known who read fiction by choice. Nobody really hung out with Eugene because he didn't try to look wealthy. Nobody really hung out with me because I was awkward and wore ratty Aerosmith t-shirts. Eugene liked that about me and would ask me questions sometimes. He would ask me if I had heard of punk rock and if I had a nuclear family. He would ask me where my dad was and if anyone ever beat on me. He would ask me if I really was gay. If I was, that's cool, because his brother was gay. And although coming out for him broke the family in more ways than one- he continued to write Eugene letters. Eugene considered him a hero.

"I guess I'm not really gay. I've never dated a girl or anything. But I think about them when I jack off sometimes."

"You masturbate?" Eugene said. "That's awesome. I always knew girls did it."

"Don't they all?"

"I think only really cool ones do. Or gay ones."

"Man, I'm really happy I'm either cool or gay."

"Seriously." He said. "Nevertheless, I'm sorry no one came to your party."

"It's okay. I don't even listen to TLC. That's all they would have wanted to listen to anyway. I think I was just scouting out talent for potential friendships, you know? They lost the audition."

"Yeah, you don't need those kids."

"I guess."

"You're one of us."

"Even if I turned out a bitch? Or a lesbian? Because I

hear I'm also pretty mean."

"My brother said gay punks always throw the best parties, and angry girls make the best girlfriends.

"Sweet. Let's hang out one day."

"Okay, but I'll have to give your record collection a facelift."

"Why?"

"I'm not telling you to burn your Metallica records; but there's this thing called punk that seems to make more sense to girls and queers than a bunch of long haired dudes jumping around and playing guitar solos. Its 1994 and there's a bigger world out there, you know."

"Okay. I'm open to change. But I doubt I'm the only girl that's into metal."

"I'm just trying to expand your mind."

"Ill expand my mind, alright. But I'm not too into the idea of smoking pot. I don't want to be a hippie or anything."

"No. You don't have to do anything. Plus, we like to go fast. I just sell weed. I don't really smoke it. But I might want to give you a haircut."

THREE

In retrospect, offhand events that penetrate our adolescence collect dust and we forget the little things that made us or broke us. Eventually, we bask in the big choices, and adult decisions live on in hearsay. Looking back, we realize, it was the offbeat instances that triggered our futures and shaped our self-esteem. Getting into fights made sense. Giving bullying punk girls with the munchies my sandwich and panhandling for lunch money made sense. Infatuations and the inability to recite them made sense. Being as timid as I was as a five year old over the subject of deadbeat dads made sense. Once I started making friends, I began to realize that kids with two parents were few and far between.

High School was a landmine, nestled in a cage of thousands. Between petty cat fights and dull lectures, I sulked in the contentment brought on to me by Eugene. Punk rock was all that mattered. It was much easier this way. It was a school in west Miami, where the students' class background wasn't always consistent, although rich kids were often obsolete. It was a school of low standards towards academics, competitiveness and sports, but with a tense embrace of social hierarchy. The student body's overall grade point average was a D.

In the outfield, the bleachers were tucked in a grassy crevice of the football field- where burnouts could coalesce.

One might often think that belonging comes with that inevitable struggle to fit in. However, in the early nineties, it wasn't cool to be uncool yet- fitting in was for the football team and the color guard. Acceptance in punk rock was based only on whether or not you show up. Show up to the show or to that comforting crevice in the outfield. We

searched for misfits and rabble-rousers- we searched for each other.

Despite our overpopulated mess of over five thousand students- things like drug culture allowed cliques to crossover. While the lively presence of other emotionally-wrecked, nonconformist teenagers provided me with safety; these were the years that strangled us haplessly. Adolescence was a disease within itself. As much as we can belong someplace, we still hate ourselves and we still have additional vices and additional drama- this justified teen-angst.

There's a percentage of teenagers who can look back at athletic highs, gossiping in the girls room, awards and accolades, and being in love with whoever sat beside them in the classroom. In most realities, this narrative was a pipedream or was so fucking normative it was everything we didn't want to be, or could afford to be. In the end, all taboos remained true; even head-cheerleaders amassed self-hate and smoked dope. They may have just not felt as malformed as the puddle of misfits who had a different take on popular culture.

The ultimate conditionings pierced into my body by high school were the need to pluck my eyebrows and to embrace academic spirit.

"How white is that?" My mother would recite. "Why shouldn't a Cuban girl be okay with her unibrow?" I fished for strength. How difficult is strength at fourteen? Extremely, I found out. I weakened and shaved the bridge between my eyes.

Within my family, beauty standards were inconsistent and flung from left to right, and from relative to relative. Within American public schools, beauty standards were polished and whitened at the seams. Girls were taught to be thin, clean, polite, and mature; no matter how many students came from Latin families. Sometimes I hated my body-sometimes I scavenged for the strength my mother talked about. However, that occasional dent in my appearance was the last notch on my list of pubescent brainwashing. Finally, I managed to romanticize not being at school. I valued the lessons on theft and finding your g-spot that I got outside of formal education. I valued the afternoons where we could ask one another questions like "What about America makes poor kids poor?" And "What's so wrong with hot girl on girl action?" We would ask questions that were taboo in mainstream dialogue. We would skip fourth period, in the park on Bird Rd., and nurse a 32oz. of beer; forties were illegal in Florida.

"You're a sell out. Last week you weren't wearing fucking khakis and loafers. Whats your fucking deal?" I asked Roberto one day.

"Whatever Cristy. In the future, when you're moshing in a pit somewhere, drunk off your ass- I'm gonna have a family. I'm gonna have money. I'm gonna be successful."

"Who are you to measure success? Youre just gonna end up fucking poor people over. You're just gonna start shitting competition from the hole in your brain your CEO job is gonna drill. You and your imaginary family can suck it."

"Whatever." He concluded.

I understood that growing up in financial disenfranchisement doesn't always allow us to idealize those dreams that involve steady paychecks. Still, in order to survive, I didn't believe we had to submit to the rich white model of success and commonality. How I would end up anywhere, without perpetuating the notion of true "selling out" was questionable at fourteen. But at the same time- ragged new belongings consumed my every fiber. And for a moment- it was the perfect assurance we needed at fourteen.

Selling out was defined by betraying the honesty and sacredness of our culture. Selling out could exist in any setting- it was any infidelity of one's personal morals.

Defying morals existed as a taboo in almost every identity I embraced; my ethnicity, my gender, punk rock. But then I would ask myself- did it make sense to defy these morals because we were broke? Did it make sense to defy these morals because we needed to heal from faltering mental health?

On one of my first months at school, I made friends and wrote a fanzine. I met a kid named Julian who also wrote a fanzine, listened to Sonic Youth, and wore a ratty Circle Jerks T shirt almost every day. I thought that was cool, so I started calling him my bestfriend. I thought if I called him my best friend enough, he would eventually become that. Fortunately, this became the case by my fifteenth birthday, near the middle of freshman year.

The people I called my friends loved life sometimes. We thought throwing rocks at each other was a good time. We sat on the grass and talked about how much The Misfits should get back together with their original singer. We sat on the grass and asked each other questions.Questions about secret lovers, ex-friends, and failed attempts at pubescent sobriety.I would open the sealed can called my father. I hardly spoke of him to my family, but contemplated openly with Julian. Julian tossed me around trash cans, and I would joke of the smell of his farts. Afterwards we would embrace and talk smack on the people who ragged on us. On good days, everyone seemed excited to be fifteen- to be growing out of a misfit shell, to be running away from home. Sometimes I adored my new changes, but at the same time, we were all understanding how our definitions of "fucked over" varied. Some of us had two parents and had been beaten on. Some of us had one parent, experienced love, but had little to no money. Some of us had no familial drama, but tied self-hate with normalcy. Sometimes I withdrew my fight. Many of us took fourteen years to realize that so many kids had it better than us. Sometimes we basked in those comparisons and the glass was always half empty. On my low moments,

I sat on the corner of the room, put my ear against the ground
and listened to the rustling and talking that seeped through
the wooden floor panels. I wanted to be alone sometimes, not
really having to talk to other people, face to face.

Freshman year, I repressed my battles. I called it
denial and everyday figured that my new loves weren't making me
stronger, but giving me the space to avoid confrontation with
real life. I was wrong for a while. I wrote a fanzine that
included narratives on why I didn't think Green Day fully
damaged punk rock because they kept this kid alive when I knew
my home-life was eighty percent heartache. I wrote about why I
thought riot grrrl was better than neo-folk feminist bands that
didn't realize how hard it is to love being a girl sometimes. I
documented pre-pubescent cock-fights I had with members of my
school's football team. I wrote about punching this gifted
student I secretly wanted to fuck. This became my nerve's
intentional retreat from turmoil.

Worrying about whether so-and-so signed to a major
label, worrying over whether or not they were going to damage
punk rock while doing so, and worrying if Janice would be able
to steal her dad's car to drive to the show beat any legitimate
concerns. I found myself concealing the questions I asked
myself daily. Questions like why did I hate some girls when the
general climate at home was anti-male? Why didn't my family
ever really talk to me about money? What was causing the wounds
on relative's skin and why didn't I know everybody's secrets?
Why did the other Latino teenagers rag on queer teenage girls?
Why did I think about people of all different genders when I
jacked off after school? Why did we stop talking about my
biological father? I didn't have my shit together- but why not
just choose to remain apathetic? After all, I did find that new
seven-inch record that gave my libido more stamina than any
adolescent jock.

Adolescence wasn't about denial, but about scavenging for potent methods of optimism and retreat. This was normalcy between me and those around me. Because we don't wake up pinpointing what brought us here, who enabled us to think what, and what should we focus on to better the unrest breaking us. We don't wake up articulating our socialization- we just roll with it.

FOUR

Later in freshman year, the boys wore a disguise of disinterest, but when they opened their mouths, they asked me about metal, mechanics, and masturbation; knowing I would answer with sincerity. That year, I wasn't about being visibly feminine and I wasn't honest about wanting to kiss both girls and boys. But with each month, calling myself a girl became less of a chore, and more of a statement of self-righteous pride. I would tell myself that maybe it wasn't girls that I hated, but any conformist behavior that dismissed the anti-hero and dismissed me. I was a person without a middle class nuclear family, I wasn't curvaceous, I wasn't emotionally intact, and I wasn't that much of a heterosexual. But while I started romanticizing teenage oddities, I began feeling like a discomfited novelty towards most boys' amusement.

"When I masturbate, I totally think about boys getting it on with each other." I said in compelling honesty.

"That's awesome." Marcos responded. Marcos was into Pantera and Women.

"Do you think about boys fucking each other too?" I asked.

"Hell no, I think about stacked Puerto Rican chicks."

"Why do you gotta say chicks?" I asked. "And why do they gotta be stacked?"

"Cause chicks with little tits are nasty."

"That's fucked up, I bet you have a small dick."

In the end, I hated those boys, but at the same time, I hated myself and my ability to be just as indiscreet. One week in my first year of high school, I devoted myself to understanding what I truly want and think, as oppose to what I'm supposed to want and think. Adolescence made our aesthetic polished and our desires tight and concise- we knew who we wanted to be. However, every bit of influence and every bit of society cramped on our identity and made whatever we wanted ten times harder- its not okay to be abnormal. So, I polished my insults and taught myself that mimicking the slander used by those around me wouldn't make me stronger, but just as tactless. In the argument with Marcos, I used the way I'm socialized to see a small penis as powerless in order to insult Marcos. So I asked myself, do I truly feel this, or am I just aware that many males in the western world are hurt by this? Do I really feel less of Marcos cause his penis might be small, or because his overt sexism is challenging my experience as a teenager? I chose the latter. I was actually terrified of big penises.

We learned about the constructs that suffocated and restricted us daily. We had questions like Why do women compete? Why do men abuse power? Why doesn't anyone think its normal that I masturbate? Why does the way I pee, the way I fuck, or the way my chest looks dictate the language that's acceptable for me to use? We aren't a malfunctioning species- were just taught to be that way.

"When the penis ejaculates, the semen enters the uterus. When semen and ovum interact, new life is created. And that's about it for sex." said my biology teacher, during a unit on sex education.

"But Mr. Rodriguez, there are more ways to have sex for pleasure than there are ways to have sex for babies. Sex may have some ancient definition that's just for baby making- but its been over a thousand years. Sex is about pleasure. Cause couples that can't make babies get it on too. We should be learning about safe ways to have that pleasure. You know everyone in this school bangs. Can we learn about STD prevention instead of babies."

"Cristy, please save this for later- this is a sex education Unit. The basis of sex is procreation."

"No, it's not. The sex you're teaching us about only talks about the pleasure of dudes. Ya'll know dudes gotta cum to make a baby, and girls don't. Teaching this way only feeds to the idea that a girl's pleasure isn't as important as a dudes. And hell knows everyone in this classroom wants to know how not to make babies as opposed to how to make them."

"Cristy, if you don't stop, I'm gonna ask you to leave the class."

"Awesome. The drugs are kicking in right now, anyway."

As western teenagers, we were challenged by constructs that penetrated our ill judgments. I began to unlearn my one-sided methods of shit talking while realizing how difficult it was to teach others. And while I learned how not to hate girls, but hate what TV had taught us- I knew one thing. I knew I hated the masculinity in boys, but adored it in the girls.

FIVE

In Miami, class and ethnicity were almost consistent both at school and in punk rock. Our backgrounds intermingled but our ambitions were questionable to one another. Our sexualities, our understanding of class, our methods of expression, and our presentation of culture was questionable. While I talked about communism, capitalism, assimilation, and preserving language- I questioned why I wasn't embracing the Latino popular culture that I felt I was supposed to. Other kids questioned why my methods of rebellion included submitting to punk rock. Punk rock, in my eyes, was a subversion of mainstream culture. But towards the kids around me, punk rock was white. Punk rock was male. Punk rock was a fraction of what was simulated on MTV. It usually involved dirty white dudes playing guitars. However, in Miami, it wasn't all so white. Miami's interpretation of punk, like school, home, or public space, was eighty percent Latino. And hell, I was into this punk rock, and I was a brown girl.

"It's the Dyke corner." A young boisterous group of girls would holler in pride at the six of us, nuzzled behind the bleachers before any of us could drive. At home, in moments on my own, the gashes ran wild and torment gave birth to self loathing. But in the arms of confidants and the stigmatized *Dyke Corner*, confidence came in occasional spurts.

"Who needs to be loved, Julian? Not me, god damn. I'm not a fucking hippie, dammit. Let's be feared." I chugged a can of grape soda after swallowing two pills of convenience store trucker speed. I ranted for minutes. "Why would anyone not want to be feared? I love the way these bitches insult us. Doesn't it just make you feel like a hardass? Damn, shit, motherfucker." Julian would interupt me with a good joke and most of us would cackle beneath our hearts. Armed with pitstains, facial piercings and bad haircuts, there was something looming, and hell knew it was killing us, yet keeping us alive.

Like my peers, I didn't want to embrace any popular culture. Still, my bind to my family was thicker than blood despite not being Latina enough to the kid that sat next to me in English class. I felt daily means to prove my roots and my upbringing, but at the same time, I felt the daily intent to prove how the energy of my wayward subculture supported me. And when school was out and mindless brawls became a repressed memory- I was finally Latina enough for everyone at the show.

Among brawls about race and punk rock, I'd usually fight back with tactlessness and profane shit. I would be irrational and not put much energy into the fight. I felt above them. Then came the point that I wasn't Latina enough to a friends mother- I was the whitish kid that would stop by every once in a while. I couldn't say fuck you- I could only sulk. My ability to hurt developed.

"So why do you listen to White music?" Tatiana asked me often.

"Why do you listen to sexist music?" I would respond.

"The Barrio Boyz aren't sexist."

"Yeah they are, they call girls bitches and hoes."

"I bet punk bands you like call girls bitches and hoes."

"No way, they call girls awesome. They say girls should beat the shit out of one of the Barrio Boyz. They can probably kick your ass too."

"I bet they're all dykes like you."

stop

**SIX**

I never really wanted to deny other kids of their personal struggles. I met girls who every football player wanted to fuck, but who probably hated themselves more than I hated myself. They feared me- for my sailor tongue, dog collars, and pit stains. But something in me kept me from coming on too strong. I could hardly abandon the truth behind our common class and ethnic makeup. Customs that consisted of a diet of pork and fried starches, and a mental pool where thick is beautiful and motherhood is revolutionary. And Cuban grandmothers. I had a syrupy romance with the cultural similarities between our grandmothers. I thought they were all the same- sweet, defiant, and loving. And while a Cuban grandmother 'aint nothing to fuck with; I wished a stout, unsure, teenage girl could have just as much power.

Sometimes I may have dreamt of everyone being a big gay underdog, but I knew the normalization of queerness in my public high school was often times implausible.

"My family are a bunch of catholic Cuban traditionalists. I can't tell them I'm okay with homos. That's wack." Angelina confessed.

"But Fidel hates homos. Shouldn't they at least want to liberate them from the shackles out of spite?" I would respond.

"Fidel also hates capitalism as much as my dad. Similarities can arise between enemies."

"But homos are different than capitalism. They're actually really cool." I debated.

Angelina was not very much like me, although, we shared an interest in speed. She attended raves before they became teenage chic. Angelina was a subculture prototype. She had almost florescent tattoos, chin-length hair that was dyed red, and strips of reflective tape encircling the seams of her pants. She would always ask me if the rigidity of my jeans ever made me unintentionally orgasm. I would always ask her if her pants were where she kept a well-concealed penis. And

for some strange reason, it felt reasonable to flirt with her.
I would occasionally stare at her breasts when we spoke to each
other. I hated when boys did the same to me- but a part of me
knew she knew, and part of me knew she liked it. She would
often flirt in return, while saying she would never want to
kiss a girl, but it was difficult for me to take her seriously.
We were too different, at any rate.

"Not all homos are cool." She rebuttled.

"Most of them are."

"Are you a dyke or something?" She asked me, and I tried
everything in my power to keep my composure, behind the swaying
mess of black knots that covered my eyes from view.

Insults were dispersed,but I slowly became immune to
them. However, freshman year, I found a muse. Everyday at noon,
I would hear songbirds and see an angel between first and
second period. And it wasn't until the third time she passed by
me that I understood the unnerving quiver that consumed me when
I saw her. She had jet black, knotted hair and the voice of an
angry sailor. She wore this tattered tericloth dress all the
time. The frayed fringe sat right above her knees. She strutted
brawn- her knees were always scabbing. She was often sandwiched
between these two boys, Lars and Enrique. They looked like body
guards, but in my fantasies, this girl fought for her self.
They were each twice her size, but the curl of her upper left
lip and the way she crushed the handles of her bag made me
believe she could beat them senselessly. Her name was Selene.
Selene never smiled at me, and I never smiled at her. It was my
method of rejecting my own vulnerabilities. She was openly,
visibly, and fearlessly queer. Everyone talked shit about her.
Because to many of the kids at school, it was common knowledge
that all dykes had five STD's a piece. To many of the kids at
school, it was common knowledge that disease that intermingles
sex is only prevalent in gay communities. In return, people
like Selene were singled out, terrorized, and tormented- our
identities were often times fractured. People like Selene

were bound with vengeance. Her heroism made me want to be her.

No matter how much I learned, self-taught, or understood how we're taught to comprise; girl socialization required years of deconstruction. My early relationships with other girls were laced with vanity and competitiveness. We were taught to pre-judge one another; hate each other, and conceal our love for each other. She dressed like me, looked like me, was bullied like me, sometimes I wanted to kiss her, but I called her a bitch because she wouldn't look at me. I thirsted for the girl-solidarity I embraced with strangers and heard of in punk rhetoric, but could never share with Selene. The songs I would hear would say that girls fought back together- but was this the truth? Or did it require more growth to abide by that? This was what I knew then. We, as the angst-ridden teenage girls, were taught complacency and susceptibility. We wanted to untie the restraints stifling our anger and unravel our ability to fight. Growing up in skin that curves dissent from the girl-stereotype meant growing up with towering defenses. My defenses came in the shape of slander and a need for others to prove themselves. Selene was like this too. And maybe it was just easier to hate Selene rather than to prove myself to her. This is where my competitiveness stemmed from.

On some nights, I found that girl-solidarity when this one girl, Marietta, sat on my bed until 3am talking about how useless facial masks and pussy deodorant were. I shared my room then with relatives, but sectioned off my side with yellow caution tape and a wall-collage of posters, flyers, and strategically placed crap. I was into dim lighting and denying others' intrusion so I could achieve a private space for writing zines and jacking off. We talked about fucking, punk, metal, crank, and weed. I didn't smoke weed at the time; I only wanted to be sociable and stay awake, mostly. On some nights, I also wanted to be skinny; but only Marietta knew this.

As a result, speed was more my style. Still, we studied
marijuana a lot, because I was intrigued by hallucinations.
Marietta knew more about inhalants than I did, she smoked
cigars. I tried to teach her how to play guitar. Marietta was
my age, into attending punk rock shows, but sometimes nothing
like me. She was hardly social, liked muted colors and heavy
metal. She thought punk rock was okay, but didn't think it had
as much testosterone as she liked. Any concept remotely
femme was inane to her. That year I began changing- I
began tampering with girl-conditions and learned to abuse them,
as oppose to completely abandon them. That spring, I learned
there was something about girls- something about their fists
when they fight and their hair when it isn't washed. Something
about the wrinkles on the corner of their eyes when they smile.
Something about their tact for defacing the rules bestowed upon
them, but still making it okay to smell like shit, and wear
that short skirt in defiance. There was something- something
about Selene.

SEVEN

Marietta was the only person who knew I ever thought of Selene in this way. Marietta was the only person who knew I didn't only want to fuck boys. At times, I wanted to be like Marietta- she got okay grades but didn't get into the trouble that I did. I call dealing with sexism "trouble". Trouble that I questioned whether or not I got myself into it. She didn't get called a slut like me. She was never asked to suck some kid's dick in the public bathroom like me. She was never called a nasty dyke. She never tried to fuck some boy because it might just feel good. In a way, I often forgot there was a part of Marietta in me, though veiled by who I thought I was. She didn't want to blame herself for being hurt by boys, tension, or vanity- she obscured any adoption of sexuality.

Sitting behind an old sation wagon on my street, me and some boyfriend kissed for hours. "This is a shameless experiment" I thought to myself and wished to never be called a slut. "I want to know what this feels like, you know, with another person." Groping his legs at nightfall, I grabbed his cock and it was the first one I had ever felt. "Lets see if I can do this" I thought again, and pressed my mouth against it, assuming it was the next obvious step. Fireflies encircled the station wagon and did a dance that made blowjobs feel a little more tender. A little more in tune with nature where the only missing ingredient was my own arousal. "Will you finger me, dude?" I said outloud, and after a second of his finger uncomfortably pulsating my pussy in a manner that hardly felt like my own, I laced my fingers around his and taught him the proper way to delve into the proper hole. "Like this, dude." The fireflies watched, hardly poked fun, and I felt victorius.

I was sexually active that year and I would confuse orgasms with love sometimes. Despite the emotional chaos that tied my heart in knots in most endeavors- lust was always

stronger than love that year. While my school was dense with
individuals, the closeness of classroom interactions made
everyone able to be up on one another's shit. Kids' inklings of
my sexual activity enabled shit talk. I told myself that I
asked for it, when a kid I'd rather spit on, tried to coerce me
into fucking. I told myself I asked for the scars, the
discomfort and the eating disorders. I told myself I asked to
be manipulated by saying "I love you". I thought declarations
of love from teenage boys justified the times they smiled at my
purging a pork sandwich, because I would finally look sexy. And
in order to not submit to a fight- I told myself Selene
probably asked for it too. We were all at fault, I thought.

It was a cycle. A boyfriend makes me feel ugly, so I,
then, hate my body; although attempt to laugh in return. I
cheat on him with another closet girl in the storage room.
Then, the football team overhears the incessant moaning- so

who is a slut? Who is a dyke? Who sees those as rewarding
traits? A fraction of my heart adored those traits. However,
despite the orgasms and the self-discovery- a fraction of my
heart hated free love and homoeroticism. After all, it is what
got the mainstream talking smack.

Gustavo asked me to suck his dick again. Do you think
I'm asking for it by being honest about how I get it on with
other people? I can't fucking deal. That kid is busted. I wanna
take a piss on his car. Have you seen that piece of shit? His
name is inscribed on the windshield in busted-as-fuck decals."

"You're not asking for it." Marietta laughed, but
sustained an ounce of concern over me. "I never thought you
were asking for it. I just think that embracing sex is what
gets dudes to fuck with you. And I just don't want to deal with
it."

"I guess I'm not asking for it. I guess I should curl up
and die and never make out with anyone again. I guess I should
rub one out for the last time before my journey to the convent,
where I'll be sewn so shut, It might even hurt to take a piss. So
what do you think? Do you think Im asking for it? Just because I
want to do it that kid who sucked at fingering me told everyone?"

"I don't think so. I just wouldn't do it."

"So I have no self-control? I want it to be okay to get laid sometimes."

That talk went in circles for years. I read about people using sex as a way of learning about their bodies. I read and listened to sermons about loving yourself and how it is, in fact, possible to be a commendable slut, because promiscuity can be achieved in healthy, consensual ways.

However, inside, I would sneer and sigh. There was a dense corner of my room, nudged between the closet door and old scraps of fabric, where I kept my stash in a plastic airplane. It was speed, titilating human fuel, handed down by Marietta's cousin. The thin line of ivory dust made a sandstorm between my nostril and my lungs. My wings spread like a moth who learned to fly days after she was expected to. I layed on my sheets, clutching the frayed ends of a ragdoll that I kept for recollection of the time none of this mattered. The pebbles on the ceiling did a choreographed dance I felt alive. I wasn't afraid of questions; I found a slight grip to the answers. When would I ever engage a teenager who wouldn't tell lies and admit to their own sexual curiosity? When would the line "Make me cum" be deemed as alarmingly beautiful? Adulthood, perhaps? Sprawled in this chemical escape, I digressed.

In the end, these were the lies that shaped our teenage esteem, and the conditions that blocked our ability to embrace our sexual selves. These were the self-deprecating stipulations that disallowed us to feel empowered by even healthy sexual interactions. We didn't ask for it, but it would take another year to believe that. My actions weren't always choices. Although one choice was consistent- that choice about who I wanted and struggled to be seen and accepted as.

EIGHT

"You should just tell her that its fucked up to say fag when you're a straight kid." Eddy told me during a fight in English class.

"Why do I have to do all the fucking work? I already have to deal with the challenge of surviving."

"So are you gay?"

"Geezus Eddy, why are you making me choose sides."

This was a common exchange during talks about queerness and how queer and self-questioning folks were always the ones teaching. In sects of the community I was coming from, groups often taught tolerance. And while these groups saw progress- queer people felt that ineffectiveness of fear.

"Tolerance is fear in disguise." I thought. Queer communities don't need tolerance, but acceptance, understanding, and straight people saying "what can I do?" What I saw weren't alliances, but queer Latinos doing the work of spreading knowledge and advocacy. And in the space and the heart of any closet fifteen year old, the platform to do that work hardly existed.

In my home our tone swerved by way of narrow traditions and belief systems. We went from talking about politicizing our choices to talking about how to raise baby parrots and make flan. At home there wasn't a space for anything remotely sexual. While my culture welcomed that political progress that entailed fighting for fair pay and abiding by self-sufficiency- the revolution wasn't very gay. Queerness seemed ten times more repressed in my cultural boundaries than that of white commercialized America.

"Why can't queers just be a hot commodity?" I asked Marietta. "You know, the way homos are in white people culture."

"Because you want to be respected for who you are, not

your novelty."

"Fake respect is better than none at all."

"No, really, it's not. Trust me."

I marveled blindly at the communities that were
exoticized in white America- "Did they get paid for this? Is
this actually positive attention? Seriously." I told myself. I
was blind and in flux. In my outside circle, we talked about
queerness. I wrote in a zine about queerness and we tried to
never assume one another's lifestyles beyond the common
assumptions. Assumptions like what music we probably listen to,
what drugs we probably smoked, and what politicians we probably
hated.

I had a pen pal from southern California named Yami. She
wrote me letters about growing up Chicana and queer. Her queer
community was mostly white, while talk of her sexuality never
went beyond that. Her mother was tighter with Jesus than Yami
was to her girlfriend, Janeane.

"How can I tell my mom about Janeane? How can I tell her
without seeming totally anti-god?" she asked me on the phone
one day.

"Tell her you met Janeane at Church."

"No, for real."

"I just don't cross that boundary. Sex talk is for
friends, prude talk is for family. It's not all a bad thing,
though."

Yami ended up coming out to her mother that spring. Her
mother blamed the white people she was devoted to. She blamed
whiteness infiltrating their community and stripping their
youth of Catholicism and spiritual growth. I learned to
understand the obstructions in my cultural settings. Though, at
the time, I wasn't afraid of queerness. Before educating myself
of any repression of queerness in Latin culture- I ruled out
whiteness from my queer community. Selene was Cuban. Eugene's
brother was Colombian. Eugene's brother was a hero and Selene
was my muse. On good days, I romanticized everything I touched.

I related queerness to that inspiration
and that offhand support given to me by those as tattered; as
dispersed.

"Go to this party with me tonight. It's a dude party and
theres this dark room with a blacklight where girls make
highlighter prints of their nipples on the wall. They keep
a bunch of blow in that room." Angelina asked me one time at
school.

"Sure. But aren't you afraid I might try to make out
with you when we're coked up in a tiny room together?"

"Not really, I might be into it."

The night of that party, there wasn't a hidden stash of
coke, but our breasts were in places besides a nipple imprint
mural. Like each other's mouths.

"So I think I'm gay, and I feel pretty okay about it. I'm
sorry if I ever gave you shit. Now its just a question of
coming out to my mom."

"And your boyfriend in the other room."

"Fuck that kid." She replied and I smiled a knowing
smile. Sometimes, we idealized the situations that make our
ability to smile less difficult. But back at school, the aura
is less ideal. The day of the argument with Eddy, I looked at
him and thought- you are straight, aren't you? How can you
support a queer person? Vouch for them? Rally for them as
someone with a lot more privilege? He would shrug and cackle.

"Why the fuck did you just sit there when she punched
Selene? I thought you were her friend." I asked Eddy.

"I know Selene okay, but that girl punched her cause
she's a dyke. That's not really my business."

"But don't you get that it's totally shitty that some
girl is gonna get punched cause she likes getting it on with
other girls?"

"Yeah, but I guess it doesn't offend me that much.
Everyone has different reservations. And its not like I'm a fag
or anything."

Most of us had a place to go home to, but Yami lost her home that winter. She said it was okay because the weather was so brisk and flawless in southern California. She said she was moving into a squat in the east side. She told me that a squat was the creation of a home in a place that is seeping with abandonment and a place that is sometimes safe. Yami was kicked out of her folks' place after being called Una Dichosa Tortillera. Vaguely, that translated into "a goddamn dyke". Yami had friends she could confide in; her squat became her new home. I thought to myself how I could never risk my home and the parts of family life that consoled me. I could never run away, I thought. I didn't trust many people, and being alone without arm-length trust gave me chills and diarrhea. I didn't understand how I could ever find lasting friends who would put me up the way Yami was put up.

Yami sent me photographs of her home. Tarlatan swathed a padlock door, weeds and daisies trickled through the floorboards, collages pivoted almost every corner of the concrete walls, and the windows and doorways were arched.

"I always wanted arched doorways." I told her over the phone.

"If you moved to California you would get year-long florida winters, duraflame lighting, a giant bag of weed, a warm place to pee, and arched doorways." she persuaded.

"That shit's so far fetched from anything that makes sense to me."

I entertained this often, but I was afraid if I went anywhere but here, some kid's mom would accuse me of being too white, and I wouldn't have the existence of people like Selene to fall back on. Anything outside of Miami seemed scary to me, I thought. Here, I was crowded by Latina underdogs, whether or not I knew how to talk to them. But maybe Yami would be my hit-woman, and I could defend myself a bit better? Then I could prove my theory that queerness was multi-ethnic, I thought. Maybe she could win her mom back, but maybe she didn't really need to.

Back home, temptation rattled, and I always found methods of leaving home. There was the girl two houses down who always smoked weed and had a great dane. I would say I was going to play with the great dane, but in reality I was eight miles away. I would see the sunset from a steep incline on the side of a pet shop in south Miami. On the side of the building there was a rusted ladder and it could hold ten times my weight. I would hung off the side and watched the clouds migrate. The building overlooked a park that always had hidden treasures awaiting the arrival of junky teenage pioneers. It had post-development leftover swamps, Spanish moss, ivy creeping up the hidden corners of banyans, and used condoms at the end of twigs. That's the park my friends and I got wasted at.

My family never told me it was okay to think I'm gay, want to have sex, get into fist fights, and stay out late. But they said it was okay to seek solace- to dismiss qualms back home and embrace retreat. They said it was okay to hate the man and love your identity- your wayward haircut and your defense of pockets in North Miami that were being fucked over by the city commission. They thought about this a lot- about people, economy, human need. So we talked about it sometimes. My mom would ask about those bohemians I said I trusted, and I would tell her that at punk shows, people weren't usually drugged and murdered like at rock concerts. I told her I was over Aerosmith and I didn't really intend to see any band that would charge a door fee more than five bucks. But then again, she and I knew that as much we can love any space- ultimate safety was a pipedream.

"If home can't be completely safe," she'd say "then why should a punk show be?"

She thought it was okay for me to find retreat that year. Home can't be perfect, but we were trying, I thought. And maybe outside influences can build on that definition of home- my mother helped out my lost teenage friends most of the time. This one night, we housed an assembly of post-show, teen-debris because all those kids could have been disowned if they dared showed up at their parent's half-drunk. It may not have been that ultimate safety, however, it was an agreeable start.

It became okay that I couldn't share my innermost feelings on oral sex, fisting, and Selene with my family. Because we could talk about other things. We could talk about our formative heroes selling out, and about cast aside neighborhoods. We could talk about dismay and how its sometimes followed by deliverance.

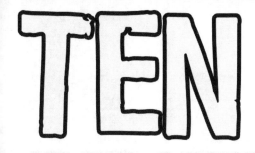
TEN

Skipping school built the
framework for loving myself.
My life within pockets of
subcultures was where
I could retreat to on weekends
and stagnant class periods.
In the world that I
fantasize of- the ability to love yourself and unlearn
oppressions can be introduced in schools. Schools can house
that retreat and undo the tensions of a kid's everyday agenda.
I thought schools could somehow abide by compassionate
intentions. However, not everyone's story sets off formal
learning as a tool that ever engaged us. And everything I
learned throughout my high school career, I learned from
skipping class.

By this point, I called someone like Julian my best
friend enough times to have my mom deem him a part of the
family. Valuing a person who lived closer than California was
new to me, but in a way, reassuring. We shared tips on
fashioning ratty clothing, outdoing facial piercings, and
wicked awkward drug stories. We shared time and honesty. I felt
this was progress. On that year, I abided by my new rules of
doing what I want and not what I'm taught; I talked to girls
other than Marietta.

I started living up to my needs and desires a little
after my fifteenth birthday. In no time, I sat in the back of
the classroom, talking about Metallica and virginity with a new
girl who I had just been transferred into my class. Her name
was Desiree. She knew Selene. Initially, I felt the rule of
transitive property would leave me, at some point, making out
with Selene under a bleacher during math class. My thoughts
were hot, but reality was dull. However, I grew close to
Desiree.

Desiree was tall, with brown curls cupping her cheeks.
She enjoyed black metal and had cigarette smoke-stained sermons.
constantly dripping from between her teeth. Desiree was from
Venezuela, rubbed off on me, and changed my regional dialect.
Over nightmares and a love of arson, she would sneak me out

of class and I tasted hard liquor for the first time with her. She often told me everything, and I mostly did the same.

"So, did you know I think I'm kind of gay? I had phone sex with a girl the other day." I told her.

"Yeah, you're totally transparent. You can shut up about it. But I don't care. I think it's hot."

"True."

"I think that kid that's trying to bone you is also trying to bone me. It's annoying. He always asks me for weed and tries to touch my hair."

"It's okay. I don't even think about him when I masturbate, but I think he thinks I wanna bone him back. Fuck a bunch of that. He told me I was fat."

"Fuck that, I can't deal with people who don't make me feel good about myself."

"Yeah. But we're young. We're allowed to fuck up sometimes."

"It's not really that way for me." She told me. "I don't want to have time to waste." This was Desiree's aphorism.

There was five kids who wore trench coats, platinum accessories of skulls, and metal-cast jewelry that was linked by bones. Once I thought they were righteous death metal dudes, but then I realized that death metal was a novelty to me and I didn't really wanna slay women and fuck 'em in a fire pit. They had facial hair and were in their fifth year of high school. They all smelled like cigarettes and gasoline. Desiree started calling one fur of yellow as an homage to his long golden tresses. They hated us. They hated angry women. They hated women enough to dedicate hours to discussion on how they were only good for fucking. They sat in the music room most of the day- peering through the windows and heckling female passerbys through homophobic, fat-phobic, sexist and ill-witted slurs.

"Here come the feminazis."

"Fuck off asshole, or I'm gonna shove your dick up your

asshole."

"Fuck you, I'm not a fucking fag, you dyke."

The kids couldn't stand our feminist "bullshit". I didn't understand the privilege of being apolitical. But in a way, I guess some kids could deem political correctness as uptight and obnoxious cause they don't gotta deal with being called a bitch or a spic every day of their life.

That year, I began re-evaluating the way I romanticized misfit subcultures. Direct solidarity among all underdogs was an often impossible pipe-dream. Unity wasn't about the underdogs locking arms- it was about the people who made sense making sense in the same room- together, safe, and drunk.

However, there was substances and calluses pulsating the binds between us. While musical values and rebellion allowed us to intermingle- self-doubt, self-hate, angst, and drugs allowed us to be. We didn't wallow in self-deprecation because it was fun, we didn't choose to be wayward, the outlandishness chose us. We said okay to it because it provided a space to bind, unwind, and seek sanctuary from everything else. I never understood outcasts who came from wealthy suburbs- what were they complaining about? But in more ways than one- substance abuse exists in a million shapes. It can be rich, it can be poor, it can make us all isolated, and it can sometimes make us understand one another better. The culture that chose us provided a space to talk about those daily battles and the daily instability that sustained our mental health. We embraced feisty pride when we could. Albeit, at night, the lights were dim, the rooms were cluttered, and every one of us looked the same, smelled the same, and were as drunk or stoned as ever.

I chose booze and speed to provide self-awareness, others chose hallucinogens as a retreat. I chose denial to feel okay, others were on bad trips and I would tell jokes to them so it wouldn't be so bad.

"It's weird that stupid jokes and getting wasted are

the only thing we have in common." A boy said to me- I never got his name.

"Yeah, I guess we wont ever be real friends. Because maybe one day I wont need this to feel beautiful."

"Um, yeah. I guess people look pretty hot when they're high."

"What?" I dropped the insightful dialogue. "I think people look like unicorns when I'm high."

"So, do you wanna take a hit of this?"

"Hell no, weed's for hippies, I just need crank. You know, we gotta go fast, ya'll gotta go slow. That's why hippies play in jam bands and punks play in punk bands."

"I think speed would make me wanna fight my dad."

"I think weed would make me think too hard about fighting my dad."

That year I learned to understand substance addictions. They weren't the choice we consciously made to promote self-help. I learned to understand how drug culture is implemented in cast-aside groups; the people with "problems". Drugs had terrorized young people who didn't have an alternative to help them cope with their own difficulties. Working beyond addictions and that vision of drugs as a final verdict was a challenge that winded us. My eyes often swelled with ache and tears. I saw kids my age in dire need of that outside substance- in need of a mind-altering answer to self-love, fascination, and impulse. In my head, I wanted to change that and to move beyond that. But I was fascinated at how distorted and obscure everything we said came off as when we were plastered. I liked the way everyone looked like an alien. It was like taking a crash course on surviving on another planet. Then, I would remember why we started chugging, snorting and toking at that age- why we hurt so bad and why we searched for that temporary numbness. Then I would remember how adolescence was like a disease in itself, and we sometimes thought we found a cure.

Within the sphere of my teenage culture, I saw suicides and self-hate, and I said this wasn't me. But who was to say that we can always find that light at the end?

There was this kid, he would pass out flyers for punk shows outside the front door for my school. He blocked the hall; his smile was bright and he took up space that would often be taken by the color guard after a less than awesome pep rally. He smiled at me and I introduced myself.

"I'm Cristy Road, who are you?"

"I'm Jaime. Come to the show next weekend."

"Okay. If Janice can steal her dad's car."

"Awesome. I'll be there. I'll see you around." I tried to walk beside him, but hordes of teenagers got in his way. I started running to catch my bus. Jamie was on a wheelchair and tried to knock over some simulation of a homecoming pep rally, but failed. He trailed behind and I waved goodbye.

Jamie wasn't at the show that weekend and I never really knew his story. A week after that, the hype after school was that Jaime took his own life. I cried a little and realized that we had that power; to hurt, question, and choose death over healing. Healing is more than spewing out remorse and asking for a shoulder to cry on. Healing is sparse and concealed. Healing is harder to come by than cheap dope, random acquaintances, and fatality.

I decided that I could find therapy within me- I could help people, I told myself. I wanted to be that redeemer - that one who meshed so well with counseling and providing a shoulder to lean on. I tried to provide sermons for my friends who needed salvation. I tried to sing them songs and write them letters and tell them how attractive I thought they were. I tried so hard I forgot about myself. And in the end, who was there for me?

The invincibility of youth often fades. When our flame of unruliness and power flickers near the end of a frayed wick, our inhibitions shined and our power dwindled. What we needed wasn't that temporary retreat nestled within a thick white line, but each other. It was always difficult to find each other.

"Should I do the rest of this? My brain is working faster than my lungs. I can feel my heart. I think I can see yours." I asked someone on one of the last times I did speed during high school.
"Yeah, please."
"Here is to feeling like shit tommorow." I celebrated.
"Isn't living fast your only option sometimes?" he said to me and smiled. "We're all gonna die anyway, right?"

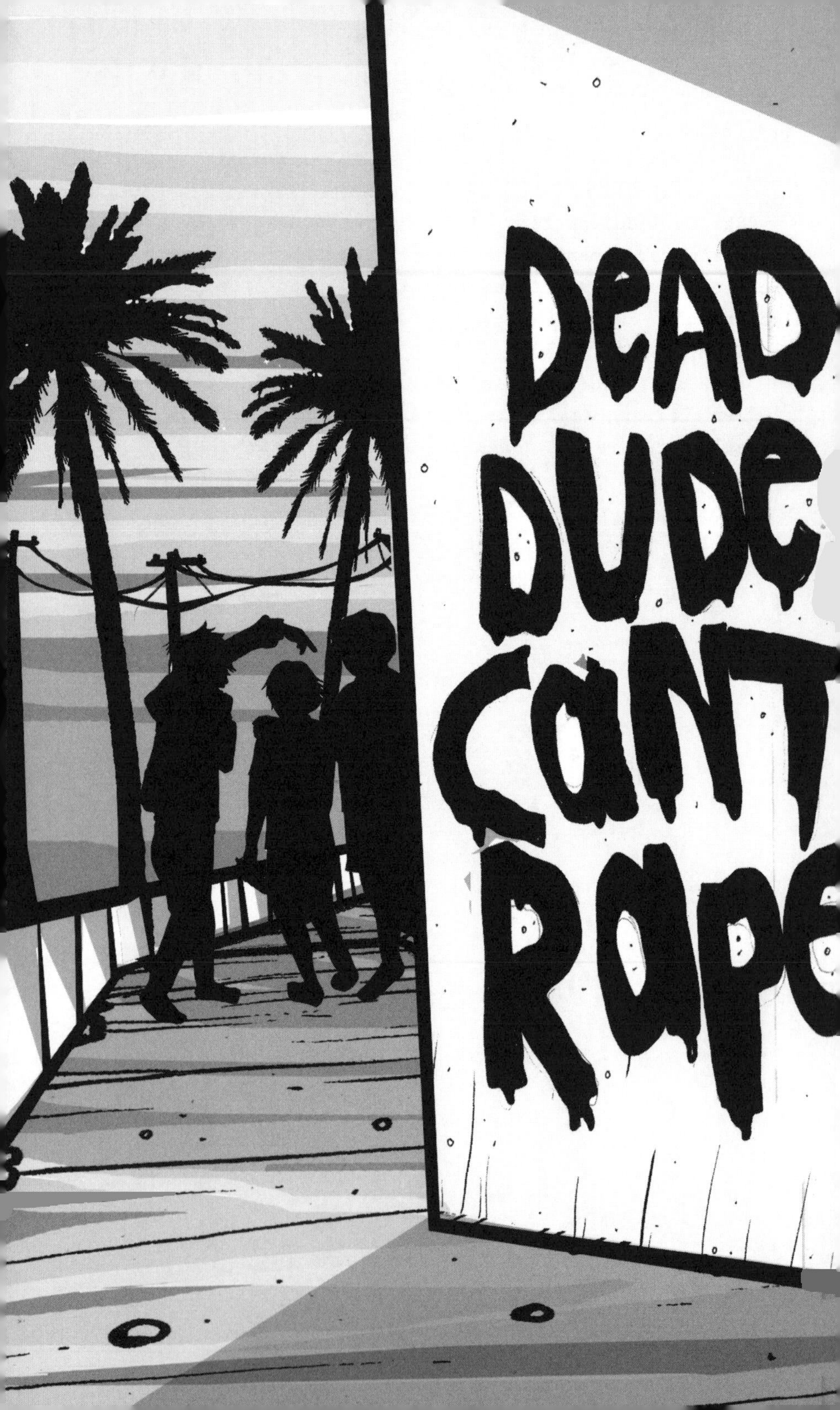
DEAD
DUDE
CAN'T
RAPE

ELEVEN

"Can you see what that sign says? I don't even know where the fuck we are. I hate house shows in bumfuck Egypt." Katlyn said while she was driving us to a show on the northeast end of Miami. It was a quarter to midnight and we passed a 24 hour mini-mart in a Haitian neighborhood. A man walked down the sidewalk and peered through the windows of the car. Katlyn hunched and swerved the car around him to take the next left turn.

"Don't hurt me, I'm just a helpless little white girl." Katlyn said to herself.

"Should we feel sorry for you?" I said to her, with cynicism.

"I'm just saying. I don't wanna get shot."

"Don't you think violence in places with lots of poor people who aren't white comes from whitey busting on their neighborhoods? You best be getting why some dude from here's gonna sneer at a white kid in a nice ass car." From the back seat, I turned to Eddy, who was sitting beside me. "Why did we get a ride with this girl anyway? She's making me wanna rip on punk kids and it's making me feel self-deprecating."

"You know your knack for invincibility always comes back to you. You'll forget her once you get home and write Yami a letter about riot grrrl and butt sex."

"I told you, invincibility isn't my goal- getting over self-hate is."

"Self-love can make you pretty invincible."

"But shit happens, you know? Self-love can break. Then you gotta learn how to love yourself all over again."

Every morning I would wake up and play "Hey Suburbia", the Screeching Weasel song. It was my power suit. Ideally, songs would give me power- songs would provide me with the vigor and strength I sought. Not speed, not co-dependency, not good masturbation- just a two minute song. But after two minutes, I'd recall the truth of how that invincibility wanes.

We would drive seventy-five on the freeway because that's how fast Julian's car could go. The resurgent appeal of growing up fast would consume us, and I'd yell something obscene out the window. That year, it was what any self-respecting Cuban girl would do- and my knees were allowed to be dirty this time. However, that spring, I broke one time. After the joyride and before the breakdown, I sat on the curb and talked about Selene, distinctly for the last time.

"Is this what our bodies are for? For getting manipulated and fucked over?" I asked Marietta.

"Why do you say that?"

"I heard Selene dropped out of school cause she got raped by some senior. I can't fucking understand why someone would think its okay to be selfish enough to rape."

Marietta embraced me, but I could only keep questioning the ideas we had talked about a year ago on my bed. How self defeating is it to develop your sexual confidence and have it torn by some dude who couldn't shove his dick someplace else? We built on our esteem for years. We created towering boundaries and defenses, we became fierce; and then the piercing incision of rape destroys sixteen years of teenage toil.

"We work on ourselves so fucking hard and then they fucking break us." I told her. "I can't fucking deal."

This was new to me. It was the first time rape had ever crossed my mind or even my language. It was the first time I reminisced and digressed over all the bouts of sexism that tortured me in the past. All their insults, all their attempts at coercion, and all their attempts at tarnishing the relationship between me and my own body. At the time, I had never been raped; but the normalization of sex as an act of control existed before me for the first time.

Selene was seventeen that year, and it was the last I had seen of her. I spent time alone every day- pacing on ninety-degree concrete, trying to sing to myself, sweating. I questioned why we didn't have this power to adore our bodies and have our inhibitions, our gestures, and our ability to say no mean something valuable. I questioned why no didn't mean anything to the kid who always asked me to fuck him after fourth period. Because "no" meant "please ask me again to suck your dick during music class". "No" meant silence. I wished I could tell Selene that "no" meant something to me; and even if I couldn't stop rape, I would try to give her bouts of power. I would be her two minute song.

TWELVE

need to support other girls and it made me grow beyond teenage competitiveness. I met a girl named Tess at a show that winter. She was a year older than me and almost a foot shorter. After a week of conversations, I loved Tess. She didn't live in my town, but we both had telephones. While dodging economic disadvantage, familial drama, unwavering self-doubt, and the seventy miles of distance between us- we lived the dream and tried to start a punk band that year.

Later that same year, I read zines by a girl named Sabina who lived several states away. I was falling in love left and right. I entertained knowing her, but hardly saw her as real; I wanted to be her, I thought. She was well spoken and beautiful- she seemed to care less about infatuations and hating herself and more about being inspired and loving herself. Her smile was always mischievous in photographs. She never seemed weak and when she spoke of sex, she spoke in a dignified grit. I didn't think I could be that confident about fucking people.

Still, by my sixteenth birthday, I felt okay- The painful nostalgia of hating my gender dwindled haplessly. I felt like I knew what I needed and like I adored what I had found. I felt like I now loved girls. I knew why It was taboo to discuss sexuality on some moments, although I still struggled with forcefully concealing it. I felt this new hope- it helped my family deal with the bullshit pressed upon them. The bullshit was only the continuation of those battles with money, deadbeat dads, and surviving in white America. I thought I could be that redeemer again. And for a day, I felt like I had forgotten the definition of turmoil.

I got to know and dissect this new dynamic of trust that existed, for once, between me and other girls.

I was reinventing these feelings of envy and potential worship for girls like Sabina. Before I called her real, let alone a friend, Sabina seemed invincible. Then we talked smack under fireflies, duraflame lighting, and the smells of sewage and crumbling sea shells. She told me of how this - and - this fucked her over and how this -and - this saved her. I told her of how small I felt that one time that this - and - this dismissed my ability to reason.

"We're disheveled and we make mistakes. We may spew self-confidence while we mix disarray with poise- but inside we're fragile." She told me, after I had read her for months, and never really thought of her as human, but an immortal heroine. I always think she was the one that got away; she moved in on me, grew at arms length distance, found love, moved on, but still checked in nine years later.

"You don't gotta forget feeling like shit in order to move on. " my friends would say. "You gotta let shit make you stronger."

I have the tendency to forget things like eating disorders and speed. To forget the economic and social brawls that fused my immediate family. To forget Selene. I cared less of interacting with anyone at school- Desiree had dropped out and Julian did too. So, while I sat in the back of the classroom writing Tess, Sabina, and Yami letters, and not so often talking, I began a process of empowerment. I stopped silencing myself and thought about how nice it would be to one day let "shit" make me stronger.

"Can you give me head in the bathroom?" Gustavo asked me for about the twelfth time that year.

"Fuck you." I said. "Get away from me."

"Come on, I heard you give head."

"Fine. Let's go. If it will make you shut the fuck up."

Gustavo smiled. I rolled my eyes. We went inside the stall in that one hallway that was diverted furthest from the main campus.

"Take off your pants." I told him.

"Yeah, girl."

"Well." I pretended to closely examine. "I don't think I can. It's kind of busted down there."

"What?"

"Yeah, I'm over it. I'm too awesome for you and you don't got game. As a matter of fact, no motherfucker in this school's got game. And if some kid tells you I've sucked a dick on campus again, I'll crush both of your skulls. And getting head won't fucking matter cause you'll be dead."

I left the stall. I said I should have done that two years ago when the banter began, but I kept reminding myself why it was okay that I couldn't. This concluded a chapter in my reputation. And from that point on, boys deciphered that the elaborated stories about how I'd fuck just anyone were often untrue. Boys only called me "bitch" now. I never knew it could even be possible. To put promiscucuity and anger on either sleeve, and use them as a weapon on the moments where inevitable human desires burn you on every end.

The discovery happened in Music Theory class. The room was in a bungalo with plastic paneled walls of formica, giving us the illusion of wood. I hated those walls; so I needed to leave every so often. The instructor was obsessed with several members of the school's chorus, so rules or assignments were far fetched. The burnouts would coalesce outside of class, pass three cigarettes around the six or seven of them in a gentler version of russian roulette. I was burned first and thought these people weren't my actual friends.

I went back to class, slouched in a carpeted, quiet corner, and nuzzled myself with headsets, a notebook, and a picture of Selene. I would listen to the occasional spurge of Pavement songs and remember what I had learned from Selene. I learned that while were all socialized to tamper with the well-being of those around us, being an us is not always what it's

cracked up to be. Growing up, we entertain thoughts of
solidarity and compassion, but a lack of constructiveness in
most teenagers is in most cases, justifiable. We're judged
poorly by those around us because we're tarnished in their
vision- loud, poor, horny, queer, outrageous. But while the
banter on what bitches we were rustles in memoirs and
recollection, we learn to grow from this, and insults fade into
ashes. We remember the way the halls reeked of perfume, and we
preferred the way the warehouses reeked of common sweat. We
remember how every day of our adolescent life was
withered with dismay, yet agitated with a warped rendition of
hopefulness.

THIRTEEN

By my second to last year of school, I had friends who were girls and people I can tell secrets to. For the first time, I could be honest, and frequently. I could be honest to those who cared and care less about those who used me for amusement. To many people, I was just talking. Talking about pussy, talking about how I adored the femininity in boys, talking about the subversion of hetero love. To most kids, being all over the place as far as choosing a gender who you wanted to fuck was a phase. The invalidation pressed on everything by my life in high school made my desires offbeat- never normalcy. This put a fault in how visible I wanted to be, so I began changing that year. I began concealing my emotions from those outside my comfort zone. I began losing acquaintances while strengthening the interactions that meant something. I began burning bridges and making new ones. I fell in love for the first time that year. His name was TK. TK became like a best friend I sometimes wanted to fuck. I talked to TK as much as I talked to Tess.

TK lived almost three hours away and called me everyday at impromptu hours. The sensation between us existed thanks to mutually favorite bands and an ability to make light of everything we touched. We helped one another enjoy life better that way. I learned that my anti-love, anti-emotional doctrine came from my resentment towards public affection. The smothering, the dependence, the lacking individuality- it made me question why people chose to commit. I would read about it and often relate it to everything that is wrong with the world. Relationships? Balls? Chains? Titles? This appalled me. Long-distance affection supported my reservations. I wanted to subvert love that year. I thought love could be something unique to what it was supposed to be, or what I thought it was.

"But love can act as a precious human condition." I

thought. "Love can be a thing we relate to passion, stimulus, communication, and getting laid. After all-" I thought "It could at least make us smile sometimes."

I saw love as unconditional fervor for a person who sang songs to me when I was depressed. I thought it was shared aimlessness and anxiety. I thought it was having my hair held back when I vomited off the 826 bridge in West Miami after a less-than-sober night of singing and dancing. I thought it was the ability to say the same joke at the same time and only make complete sense to one another, but seem like aliens to those around us. I thought it was sex in a public bathroom because we could only meet halfway and could hardly afford a motel. I thought it was waking up beside them, wiping the donut off their chest, and resting my head on them. I thought it was making first moves that could get me in jail- or at least the hospital. I thought it was enveloping the petty beauties of restless teenage hood and adoring life, triumph, and failure. Together.

Love has evolved into the ability to romanticize the same interactions, but follow them with questions about how we can make love support one another and how love tortured us. Love is and was seeing our weaknesses as normalcy and our strengths as compelling. Right now, it's talking about how I'm still capable of hating myself at times, and talking about how they help me love myself at other times. At sixteen, love was only the latter- love used denial as a form of salvation. Love could still be feeling like I got the worse end of a fight, but hearing them tell me that I still looked beautiful. Love was sharing what the deepest wounds meant. Now, love is allowing those wounds to scab and heal. Love was talking about connections; now its talking about those connections, compassion, consensual sex, and privilege. Love was and is acknowledging the need for space and personal growth. Talking sometimes, leaving one another alone sometimes, missing one another sometimes.

FOURTEEN

The spring before I turned seventeen, my house often
smelled like artificially scented soaps. It smelled like
genetically engineered pears and raspberries. The smells
reminded me of something youthful; something effervescent and
new. Doubt withered with winter and the heat put me in a choke-
hold. I was manic. I hadent seen a spring as damp in over
three years. The fog and gray inspired me- I always wrote
about the new love and romanticized the existence of my band
that never played shows. The sun wasn't out to fry my brain,
the fog was out to cloud it. Those six months of manic joy made
me feel and look high almost everyday. I left my house often
that year. The air would tickle my skin and I would reiterate
that I was finally happy to be this version of a girl, after
all these years. I would wake up ecstatic sometimes. I didn't
need crank to enable this, only determination. And while my
ability to remain ecstatic was consistent, my ability to break
into shambles of self-doubt was almost as consistent.

"You're really bipolar." Marietta told me.

"No, I'm not, shit just sucks sometimes and other times
it makes me feel like I'm on crank. Except the enthusiasm that
lasts for months doesn't fuck up my teeth. Which is great,
because I still haven't been to the dentist."

"No, I'm serious, you should see a doctor."

"But I really like the days of propelling enthusiasm. I
get shit done."

"You always get shit done. Remember that month that your
life was exactly the way it is now except you hated everything?
You made seven three-foot by three-foot paintings. It was
wack."

"I think the months where I lose it, like that, are the
months where I'm open to myself. You know, about the way my
life isn't perfect."

"But don't you want balance?"

"C'mon Marietta, balance isn't punk."

For myself, then and now, there was never any gray area.
Although my months were sectioned off into black or white, the
nooks and pockets that lay between brilliance and madness never
saw that gray area. My diagnosis was never tampered towards
meds and psych wards; I kept quiet. I liked the lapse of static
and electricity. I caressed intensity, but every aspect of
hate, romance, production, and both visible and invisible
change performed these polar opposites. The polarity didn't
only exist every six months, but in my every nerve and every
minute. I hated the ends of distress; the dark ends. But I knew
it could be worse, it could be gray.

That year, the talks within my family about deadbeat
dads, abusive marriages, and slicing our incentive swelled. My
house was small, and my family was loving. It was the eighth
house I had lived at since I was born, and like my other
houses, commotion was intact and noise consoled me. Noise went
hand in hand with optimism, familial support, and domestic
chaos.

In the middle of a wave of my naively upbeat
disposition, a relative that lived with us found tumors in her
uterus. Eventually after, we found out they were benign, but
this was followed by a series of surgeries and rehabilitation.
The lapse of time created more tension, however, the new focus
was on survival. Who's to let a slew of deadbeat dads rain on
our parade, right? My family rejoiced that spring.

With the news of benign tumors, came that spark I used
to carry once, when my friends were junkies and together, we
hated the world.

"I want to be that redeemer again." I thought. "I found
something so precious and I want to share the vitality it

gives me with those around me. But how foolish," I thought.
"Punk rock and best friends isn't gonna save anyone but me."
However, it worked for a short period of time. And through that
period of time, I took what didn't kill me and let it make me
stronger. And my recipe of salvation wouldn't work for someone
recuperating from a disease. It wouldn't work for someone whose
goal is to receive adequate child support. It wouldn't work for
someone who defines survival as financial stability. And I took
that knowledge and marveled at the concept of "to each their
own." However, if a 2-minute song will make my mother smile
because she knows it will make me smile- I will play it on
heavy rotation for her if she's ever hurting. That spring, my
youthfulness consumed our living room, and triumph thickened
in my family's house.

My subculture wasn't out to prove compassion without
limitations. My subculture was never perfect, but for me- it
gave me that extra push. That belonging we sometimes need in
order to unveil ourselves when the world out there translates
into perpetual fear and rejection. By my seventeenth birthday,
we would walk in the rain and await a ride home after three
hours of drinking and dancing to some bands. I would thank
those around me for giving me support. Sometimes it didn't
matter that we weren't out to prove some revolutionary
dichotomy, sometimes it just mattered that something was
keeping us alive. We would talk about our families, our
fourteenth birthday, our bad habits, our deadbeat relatives,
and how, yeah, it's actually okay to be gay in West Miami. We
talked about the present; about how once you survive one
hellish skirmish after another, day to day survival becomes a
pretty legitimate revolution. And, in the words of my power
suit - "We won't end up like you want us to be, but so
what 'cause we're always gonna be happy, 'cause we don't
give a shit about tomorrow".

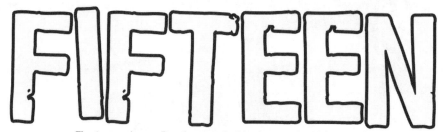

FIFTEEN

That spring, Desiree visited me sometimes, but each time, she talked less and less of what went on when I wasn't around. We went to a punk show one night, and I remember thinking hard while watching her, from dusk until midnight. Her smile, her rage, and her knack for movement and aggression. She had the energy I could only dream of. That night we sat outside of a show while it was almost ninety degrees out. She said she had been going in and out of hospitals. She told me about her conditions and the processes she was going through. She joked around their reality and compared tubes that were surgically inserted into her body to dicks.

"Look at this, it's so stupid." She'd often say.

"It's alright cause that bag totally looks good and it cancels out any fashion faux-pas."

"Yeah, I asked for it in other colors but those fuckers were all 'its not like we're the mall.' Doctor jokes are so busted."

"Doctors don't have a sense of humor cause they're sniffin' placentas all day and the left sides of their brains turn numb."

"Doctors talk a lot of smack. I overheard one tell my mother that I was dying from a disease." She laughed. "Honey, I'm not dying from a disease. I'm just living with one."

Desiree was born with a lung condition that didn't grant her a lifeline past eighteen years, unless she received a transplant. We never talked about it, although its existence was a consistent theme throughout our friendship. I didn't look too much into it, however I tried to support her in ways that I could. She gave me inside jokes, whiskey, and a slap of reality, and I gave her a shoulder and listening skills.

"You can't live life like you're pretending everything is okay. That's not truly healing. You have to confront the bullshit, only with bravery. That's the difficult part. But it makes way for some damn good optimism."

"I guess. I forget shit sucks sometimes. Petty joys like punk shows and my tight circle envelope me, and I feel like an asshole or a four-year-old. And I think that's what I mean by saying that I'm not fixing any problems."

"But if the petty things have some validity in redeeming you, than its okay. You just have to let the petty shit give you that bravery. And in the end, shit's not so petty."

"I feel like I should be sadder or strung out sometimes, like when I was thirteen. I feel stupid spreading sunshine to people who have real problems when my sunshine is just shit left behind from a really good show, or a really good fuck. Cause that hardly facilitates my healing when I'm fucked."

"But you obviously have that bravery. That ability to support or heal"

"But just cause of some stupid shit. So it just isn't as real seeming, you know?"

"Don't be so hard on yourself. Aren't you happy you have those things to live for? Aren't they allowing you to cope with these 'real' dilemmas in a real way?"

"So it's okay that stupid shit saves me sometimes?"

"It isn't stupid shit if it can keep you alive."

Our talk went in circles. I was stubborn, but Desiree showed me how it was okay to be me. She loved herself more than anyone I had ever known. Our petty highs were evident at opposite times, so we did good at keeping each other happy when the other was sad. However, one month later- we had quit the

rhetoric on retaliation. I hadn't seen her in over two weeks, though one night, Desiree had called me, laughing from a hospital bed, over a fight she saw on a daytime talk-show. She said it reminded her of the time a girl tried to slam me in the face with a math book because she thought I was hitting on her. The morning after that, my mother got a phone call from her mother. Desiree died of a lung failure on a Sunday morning.

I was crying myself to sleep again, like in the stories I had told her about being really depressed. Except this time, I learned to treasure the stupid shit. I felt like it was okay to make that rash decision to stay up for two days and start an impromptu punk band with your neighbor and their dog, solely for the sake of it making us smile. In regards to petty joys providing deliverance- I knew what she meant all along now. Anything that could defer pain and not kill me in the process was legitimate therapy.

Death was a difficult concept. I couldn't really talk about it, I could only think twice as hard. Desiree was my age, she cherished the same thoughts as me and hated the same system as me. Death and disease was for older people who were ready, I told myself. But a few hours after I had found out, I thought, Desiree was ready for anything since the day I had met her. Desiree was fierce. I learned about survival from her. For me, she reinstated that value in defiant survival, that's often dismissed as precious and worthwhile.

I grew to see my friends and I as young and powerful, but not quite invincible. For once, I didn't need invincibility. For once I realized that as real as our hurt is-fearlessness can be just as real. Invincibility was an attribute we entertained; as radicals, as manic depressives, as optimists, as romantics, and as young people with whirlwind dispositions and fucked up experiences. But a boundary exists between what's true liveliness and what's unreal. What's tactical thrill and what's naïve idealism. I never saw myself teasing or pressing a fingertip towards the edge of that boundary; Not then, not ever. "I'll be an idealist or a pessimist", I thought. Until one day, Desiree taught me about the difference between truly living and just staying alive. While you're truly living, you face danger's coils with spirit. You create emotional weapons and valiant tact.

When you're just alive, you choose an unreal outlet to avoid distraction, whether the distraction is too positive or too negative. You wallow in mediocrity and evoke simplicity. Denial makes sense to you.

My friends and I talked about this that summer, right before my last year of high school. Now, we had learned, we were living. Desiree empowered me as much as someone could.

That empowerment swerved its way into me by way of those things I wasn't supposed to be. If bad reputations and fucking in public bathrooms can lead you to self-love, the ability to understand your sexuality, and an ability to not constantly fear being poor or abused, then I carried little regrets.

"I think I found a bright side," I often thought. "I mean, we haven't self-destructed at seventeen. We must be doing okay for never having had a normal haircut, a clear conscience, or rich parents." I didn't end up with Selene, I didn't learn how to constructively mangle our differences overnight, and I was seventeen and still hovered shamefully over the topics of my own sexuality and getting it on. But I knew the sky was the limit to an indefinite number of mistakes, brilliance, girlfriends, boyfriends, delight, and squander. Success was redefined this time.

Growing up happens within each heartbeat. We can't bestow, let alone understand, our changes, although they trigger our every gesture. We learn a lesson from every mistake, every apology, every assumption at love, every new friend, every lost friend, every reconciliation, every death, every bout of belligerence, every bad decision, every kiss, every fuck, and every failed attempt at starting that stupid punk rock band. And while we abandoned the idealizing of adolescent outcast culture, a harmless identity was still, never meant to be. And it wasn't invincibility, but we were surviving outside of those conditions we had fought off for years. In the end, we remained poised while doing what we were never meant to do. And people often told me that teenagers were never meant to love themselves.

Autographs

CRISTY -
YOU'RE WEIRD AND
YOU SMELL BAD!
BUT YOU WERE
FUNNY IN CHEMISTRY
CLASS! SEE YOU
IN THE SUMMER
MAYBE! ♡
— JESSICA

Look, I'M GONNA MISS
YOU WHEN YOU GROW
THE FUCK UP AND
START A BETTER BAND
WITH SOME OTHER HOE.
BUT FOR NOW—I LOVE
YOU. CALL ME 2NITE.
        YOUR BABY'S MOMMA,
              TESS

CRISTY—
YOU KNOW I
WANTED TO GET
IN SELENE'S PANTS.
DON'T EVEN FUCKING
FRONT, GIRL.
        — ENRIQUE

STOP prank
calling me,
you bitch!
— MARCOS
P.S. STACKED
BITCHES rule!

S. RILEY—
STOP USING DOWN'S
SYNDROME BOOK BY
FUCKED YOUR
BRAIN! I'M A
PINK SHIT IS
PUSSY'S ARE SHUNS

YOUR ASS IS
GNARLY,
GIRL! LOVE,
      GINA

Have a cool summer!
Don't get so high
all the time!
        — Jenmin

fuck a bunch of that kid. You were
always the stronger one and I'm
sorry about your friend. You aren't
busted at all. — Jenna

IM HAPPY YOU CALLED ME YOUR BEST
FRIEND that one tmp. IT DID A work
a little, you know love you, honey.
        — JULIAN

C.C.
I don't
know if you
care but I always
secretly thought you
were cool. and I mean
a lot. and it never
did that but got
nice. He never tried me as a
after that X
        — John M.

PEN15
forever

Autographs

Hey, ~~████~~
Whats up? I hope
you have a - Shit,
where was I? oh
yeah. Happy
new year!
Love,
Evgene

SLUT
—Gustavo

↑ I jacked the
yearbook from
Gustavo. Fuck.
look at that
little bitch. Whatever.
I hope you have a
really cool summer.
Fuck a buncha nazi
Math teachers!
METAL **RULES**

GIRL YOU LOOKED
GOOD THAT ONE
night seriously.
ummm... What
are you doing
tonight?!?
WITH ME?
for sure!
♡ ANGELINA

CR—
MEET ME IN
THE DUMPSTER
BEHIND THE
LIBRARY. I
MISS YOU.
♡ TK JONES '98

I always
talked so much
smack on you cause
you weren't edge and
you ate my cookie the
day I met you. But you
repeatedly let you
girls can't beat me tonight
me wrong I let me realize that I can be
to a right thanks. I mean it. Call me
Love,
eddy edge

Dude I'm so
stoned! Uhh...
What are you doing
tonight. Have a good year!
uhh... yeah that Man-o-war
concert we went to was pretty
FUCK ASS HUH?!?
—Billy Razor

RISTY—
I ALWAYS KNEW THAT YOU WERE
GONNA MAKE IT THROUGH THIS
YEAR. YOU WERE NEVER ASKING
FOR IT. THOSE 3RD PERIOD BITCHES
WERE ASKING FOR IT WHEN YOU
PISSED IN THEIR GATORADE BOTTLE
+ TAGGED UP GUSTAVO'S BUICK.
OH YEAH, AND WHERE THE FUCK
IS MY KMFDM SHIRT, ASSHOLE?
—MARIETTA.

GIRL,
Yo, what the fuck?
you coming tonight
or what? IT'S
five bucks.
seriously.
Have a nice
summer.
—TATIANA

Stay Cool!
Even though I
think you're mean!
—Katlyn

BURNOUT CORNER #1

THANK YOU

To all of my friends who put blood, sweat and tears into
posing under my shit-faced supervision so I could draw
them for this novel; Aimee, Amy, Ben, Gabriel, Gloria,
Haley, Jenny, Jordan, Julia, Kane, Mindy, Pooja, Sasha,
Stewie, and Tom . To my friends in high school without
their pseudonyms.   To my friends now who enabled any act
of getting this far without completely losing it. To
        Microcosm for putting this out. To pipe
dreams, dime bags, real friends, pre-marital sex, and
people who are living their lives and not just capitalizing
    off other people's struggles.
        To growing up with grace and beautiful imperfections.

Sorry to this one old friend who I don't really talk to
so much anymore. You strikingly look like one of the
characters in this novel, but really, it wasn't
intentional.

No thanks to anyone who has tried us- To anyone who has
challenged our existence as teenagers, queers, boozers,
users, underprivileged, over stimulated, responsibly
promiscuous, and irresponsibly defiant.
No thanks to anyone who told me it was dangerous to like
    any rock band, vice, friend, or lover too much.

This story is dedicated to those who I lost,
    yet made it clear that they would never give up.

You can find Cristy C. Road and all her other projects at
                                    CROADCORE
                                c/o Cristy C. Road
                                    PO Box 60169
                                Brooklyn, NY 11206
                                www.croadcore.org
                                croadcore@yahoo.com